Charli

MW01108504

a xave ju...,

Adolfo

Before the
Night Comes

Also by Adolfo Quezada

Compassionate Awareness

Radical Love

Sabbath Moments

Loving Yourself for God's Sake

Wholeness: The Legacy of Jesus

Walking with God

Goodbye My Son, Hello

Rising from the Ashes

A Desert Place

Heart Peace

Of Mind and Spirit

Through the Darkness

The Teachings of Jesus

Transcending Illness

Old Soul, Young Spirit

A Grief Revisited

Praying to an Unknown God

Before the Night Comes

Living in the Light of
A Terminal Diagnosis

Adolfo Quezada

Dedication

To those who suffer daily from chronic or terminal illness. May relief fly swiftly to your side.

Contents

Acknowledgments

Editors are the unsung heroes of the written word. No matter how good or bad an original manuscript is, they can make it better. I am grateful to those who were kind enough to look over this manuscript and to offer me their suggestions for improving it. My wife Judy has been the one whom I've trusted over the years to give me honest feedback on the first draft of anything I write. She has a gift for spotting the superfluous and highlighting the essential of a manuscript. I thank my friends Steve Auslander and Sam Negri, who encouraged me to elaborate on and clarify portions of this book, and who used their professional editing skills to smooth out its rough edges. My friend John Miller also took the time to read the manuscript and suggest grammatical changes. Thank you all.

Preface

My hand is shaking a little as I write these words. I just got off the phone with my doctor. After evaluating my routine blood test he is concerned that I might have cancer of the blood and bone marrow.
Adolfo Quezada

These are the first words in the journal I have been writing in the months since my diagnosis of terminal cancer and which I have included at the end of this book. I wrote this book to record the transformative effect that the receipt of a terminal diagnosis has had on my daily life.

Receiving a terminal diagnosis, even before the start of any major symptoms, has transformed what had been a mere philosophical understanding of my mortality, to a concrete awareness that I will probably die sooner than I expected.

But, although I have an incurable cancer called Waldenstrom's macroglobulinemia (WM), I won't be dying anytime soon, according to the doctors who are attending me. They tell me that WM grows very slowly – until it doesn't. Right now I am not yet experiencing the symptoms that will eventually accompany the cancer.

The good news about WM is that, because it is slow to become symptomatic, those who have it are able to lead normal, active lives until the cancer becomes aggressive. For those patients who are not symptomatic, the standard procedure is to wait and watch until symptoms develop.

For my part, I do not plan to sit around waiting and watching. Of course my cancer will be regularly monitored by my oncologist, but I will be busy living my life with renewed vim and vigor.

With this indolent type of cancer it is possible that I may live for years without needing treatment.

Because of the extended prelude to death, it is even possible that I will die from something other than WM.

To be sure, the night will eventually come; but this book is about my life before the night comes. It is about the precious time that I have been granted to live and love, laugh and cry, serve and be served, and commune with God and God's natural world.

At this juncture of my illness, I know absolutely nothing about the pain and suffering, the indignity and humiliation, and the loss of physical functionality and mental faculty that may eventually come as a result of the cancer. I can't even imagine what those in the thick of their symptomatic cancer are experiencing right now because, at this point, my symptoms are latent.

Eventually, I will know the symptoms well, but at that point I may not have the capacity to write these words. That is why this book does not focus primarily on the physical effects of the cancer itself, but rather, on the spiritual and psychological effects with which my terminal diagnosis has already graced me.

I am writing this book now because some of the possible symptoms associated with WM include confusion, mental and physical fatigue, and visual loss. All of those symptoms will preclude reading and writing as well as other activities. So instead of a blow-by-blow account of the cancer's physical progression, this book focuses on my response to the diagnosis, and on how it has already affected the way I live.

Although this book includes the concepts of death and dying, it is more about life and living in the light of a terminal diagnosis.

My class in elementary school used to play musical chairs. I didn't know exactly when the music was going to stop, but I knew that it was going to stop. That was enough for me to pay special attention to the moment before me. I dared not miss the occasion. This is how it is with a terminal diagnosis. I know death is coming relatively soon, but I don't know exactly when. Consequently, I am compelled to live every day as if it were my last.

Even without symptoms, it was enough for me to receive a diagnosis of incurable cancer for my life to be dramatically affected. It forced me to come to my senses and to begin living from my basic self.

The actual day of my death doesn't have to be immediate or imminent in order to impact my life. Just knowing that my life will be much shorter than I had previously anticipated is enough to make me treat my remaining time with careful attention and profound respect. My awareness of impending death opens my heart toward others with forgiveness, acceptance, and understanding.

The diagnosis essentially stamped me with an expiration date. It's true that I have always had an expiration date - we all have - but now I see death on the horizon, and it's coming my way. Now death is no longer a philosophical consideration; it is a reality to which I must adjust. It seems the shorter my life span, the more pertinent my conscious living becomes; and the more important my need to live and love wholeheartedly.

In the months since my diagnosis, I have come to realize that, it is one thing to know existentially that I am mortal and must someday die, and quite another to know experientially that my death is relatively near according to a medical diagnosis. In the former case, I assumed that I had time on my side, and probably plenty of it. I took life for granted, and I did not realize that it could run out when I least expected. In the latter case, I am constantly conscious of – not obsessed with - my mortality.

For me, there is a dramatic difference between being conscious of my mortality, and actually receiving confirmation from an oncologist that my cancer is incurable, and that there is an approximate period of survival.

Here is an example of the difference a terminal diagnosis has made in my life.

No matter how hard I tried to die to my worldly attachments (material possessions, approval of others, accomplishments, etc.), I had remained attached. In fact, some of my attachments had become my gods. Yet, in the time since I was diagnosed with incurable cancer, my attachments have fallen by the wayside. I take no credit for it because it just happened. It happened as suddenly as if a cable between me and my attachments was cleanly severed.

I still appreciate nice things, but I can take them or leave them. The same is true about accomplishments. It's fine if they happen, and it's fine if they don't. As to the approval of others, it is no longer necessary, and it certainly doesn't motivate me.

What really surprised me after my diagnosis was my detachment from God. This may sound contradictory to everything I wrote in this book about faith, prayer, and God-consciousness; but it's not. Let me explain.

Detaching from God was not something I did consciously or purposefully. Rather, it was the natural consequence of detaching from my will. The God I willed my God to be was my conception, my creation, my concoction. *That* is the God from which I detached. What is left is the God that actually is, regardless of my will; the God to which I can neither attach nor detach because I am one with God.

I've always known that because life is terminal, I will eventually die. So why write another book about death and dying? I wrote it because, although I already knew that the Grim Reaper had promised to visit me someday, now I hear the Grim Reaper knocking on my front door. Knowing *that* I am going to die is common knowledge, but knowing that I am going to die relatively soon is a different story, a story I want to tell.

I don't really think of death as the Grim Reaper. Although death does indeed reap the souls of humankind, I don't consider it grim. On the contrary, metaphorically speaking, I see death as the handmaiden of God that comes to escort me to the ultimate dimension of life.

I have awakened, perhaps for the first time, to the preciousness of life and to my inherent obligation to live it to the best of my ability. Externally, my life has not changed much since I received my diagnosis. Internally, however, it has changed dramatically. I may be doing some of the same things as before, but now I do them from a different perspective.

> What is this state I call my Life? Is it merely a dream? Will I come to know its secret? It is so fragile, and yet so vital; ethereal, yet rooted in the depths of my soul. Life, I barely know you, yet you hold me in the palm of your hand.
>
> Elusive, unpredictable Life; fulfilling, joyous Life, you are pain and you are ecstasy. You span the eons that have been and are yet to be, but it is in the present moment that you manifest through me.
>
> Life is but a fleeting moment on the clock of eternity, yet, it is all I have. Let me awaken and live Life to the fullest. Let me not waste a moment of this precious time in stagnant slumber. Life is gift. I cannot create it – yet, I am ultimately responsible for it.
>
> In compassionate awareness, I respect Life from its inception to its

conclusion. It matters not who carries the life force or for how long; every life and every moment of life is precious. (Quezada, Adolfo. *Compassionate Awareness: Living Life to the Fullest.* Paulist Press, 2008).

Diagnosis

*What I quickly learned after my diagnosis
is that the world of a cancer patient has
many parts and a good deal of uncertainty.
Tom Brokaw*

I was surprised by my reaction to the news of my terminal diagnosis.

My world did not come to a standstill, when my oncologist told me I had incurable cancer, and I didn't become alarmed. Instead, a strange calm came over me. It was as if I had been through this before and knew what to feel and what to do in light of this life-altering development. It was as if I had been conditioned to treat illness and death as friends instead of enemies.

The oncologist checked my blood, performed a bone marrow biopsy on me, and had me undergo a bone scan. At first, he told me that I had multiple myeloma (MM), a cancer of the bone. After explaining the nature of MM, he asked me to return in a few weeks. I accepted the diagnosis and went home to prepare myself psychologically and spiritually to die.

At our second appointment the doctor told me that I did not have MM after all. Instead, I had Waldenstrom macroglobulinemia (WM), a cancer of the blood and bone marrow.

As I sat in the doctor's office trying to adjust to the new diagnosis, he presented me with yet another piece of baffling information about the diagnosis. He told me that, although I had terminal cancer, the onset of serious symptoms might not occur for some time, perhaps even years. I had readied myself for the worst scenario, but now I was being told that I had to wait, perhaps for an extended time, before I would have to address the effects of my cancer. I left his office totally confused and frustrated. My initial calm composure was beginning to unravel.

As I struggled to understand my condition, I asked rhetorically, *"Well, am I sick or not? Do I or do I not have cancer?"*

The vagueness of the amended diagnosis frustrated me - not because I had cancer - but because I didn't have cancer; or rather, I did have cancer, but not just yet; or I did, but in name only. The real cancer would come much later.

My reaction to this perplexing diagnosis was unreasonable. In retrospect, I think it had to do with losing control over the script I had been writing about my death. Cancer had deprived me of control over my health; and now it was depriving me of control over the timing of my illness. Never mind that the cancer was here to kill me, what frustrated me the most was my lack of control over the whole thing. The news that the cancer would not become symptomatic for an extended time should have elicited my relief, but instead I was frustrated. I was all dressed up with nowhere to go.

Then I decided (intellectually at least) that since the cancer would not begin in earnest for quite a while, I would just ignore the diagnosis altogether. I would live as if I had never been diagnosed with terminal cancer in the first place. This worked for about five minutes. Then depression set in because, at the unconscious level, I felt stuck. I could not really live as if I was sick, but, at the same time, I could not really live as if I wasn't. I found myself in limbo. It was like standing under a ton of bricks that would eventually fall on me, yet not being able to move out from under them.

In an attempt to control my environment and my destiny, I proclaimed to myself and others that I would opt out of any cancer treatment altogether. I had researched the trajectory of my particular type of cancer and the recommended treatments. It all sounded horrible. I concluded that the treatments would be worse than the illness, so I would just pass on them. I have since realized that any such decision needs to come after I have learned about the pros and cons of each treatment. I still intend to be very selective about what I allow to be done to me, but at least now I am open to the use of drugs, especially for palliative treatment.

I was conflicted through the days that followed. On the one hand, I wanted death to hurry and come so I wouldn't have to prolong the pain and suffering. On the other hand, I wanted to live a long time so I could be with my family. It became apparent to me that, although I may have been at peace with dying, I still needed some work with living. I was willing to die, but I wanted it to happen on my terms and according to my expectations. I had told myself that I was open to whatever came, yet, I had questions. I wanted to know when, where, and how the disease would progress. I wanted to know how long I had to live. I wanted to know exactly how the treatment would affect me.

I went into a research frenzy. I read everything I could find about Waldenstrom macroglobulinemia. (See Appendix A.) There wasn't much because WM, a lymphoma, is rare. There are less than 1,500 WM cases diagnosed annually in the United States. I searched the Internet and read book after book about lymphoma and its symptoms, treatment, and prognosis. I conferred with my primary care doctor about it, and read the latest information about the drugs currently being used to treat WM. Half-jokingly I told myself that I was acquiring more knowledge about the cancer than even my oncologist had. Fortunately, my reading also included spiritual books. I came across the following quote by one of my favorite authors, Thomas Merton. His words reminded me of something I had forgotten.

You do not need to know precisely what is happening, or exactly where it is all going. What you need is to recognize the possibilities and challenges offered by the present moment, and to embrace them with courage, faith, and hope.
                                    Thomas Merton

Perhaps recognizing the possibilities and the challenges that will continue to come in the wake of the cancer diagnosis will be my most difficult task. It will require that I recognize the possibility of pain and suffering as well as the possibility of spiritual growth and a deeper understanding of life and death. It will require that I stop to pray and meditate often and regularly in order to tap my source of courage, faith, and hope.

When all else fails, prayer and meditation are my go-to place. From deep within me came the answer to my conundrum: *Walk into the unknown with love in your heart and the rest will fall into place.* That counsel helps me to focus on the present moment and on what I know to be, and not to look into the future which remains unknown to me.

Life happens only in the now. Whether I go forward or backward, I miss out on this precious moment before me; and I miss out on life.

The diagnosis has reminded me, in no uncertain way, that there are some things I can control, and some I cannot. As I release my fixation on how things ought to be, I open to the inevitable; that which will happen despite my attempts to control it.

Because I do not know what lies ahead, I remain open to possibilities. I don't have to anticipate the future with fear and trembling. When tomorrow becomes today, I will know, and I will deal with it then. I am moving into the realm of not knowing.

Throughout my life, having control over my body has been very important to me. Now, slowly but surely, I have to give up that control. Not only will medical personnel have access to my body; poking it, examining it, and otherwise treating it as an object; but my body itself will have to give up control to the cancer as it runs its course through me.

Helplessness hurts. I know that those who love me will be gravely affected by my illness and subsequent death. Their torture will be to witness my inevitable pain and suffering without being able to alleviate it. In this sense, it can be said that my loved ones will participate emotionally in my dying time. I am in awe of how love and compassion can move mountains as well as hearts. It confirms for me that we are all one, and that what happens to one of us happens to all of us.

Sometimes I feel helpless in the light of my terminal diagnosis. But the truth is that I am not helpless. If helplessness means that I lack power to act; am weak and dependent, without protection; and am incapacitated and deprived of strength; then I am *not* helpless. Of course, I will not be able to cure my illness, but I am not helpless. I *am* able to help myself emotionally and spiritually through prayer and meditation. I *am* strong in spirit. I *am* protected from despair; and I *am* capable of enduring the pain and suffering that may come.

Of course, at this point this may be only wishful thinking. Whether I will still feel courageous, faithful, and hopeful in the midst of the actual illness, remains to be seen. But of this I am certain: all that I need is within me ready to be evoked through prayer and meditation.

Expectations get in the way of living and dying freely. I may have good intentions as I plan my dying time, but charting the future is for fools. Instead, I will live as I will live, and I will die as I will die; and all the plotting I do will ultimately be in vain. Rather than focus on how I will live my dying time, I focus only on how I am living the moment before me.

Living consciously in the present moment keeps me aware of my mortality. When I experience how fast the present moment passes into history; I realize that my life is made up of these rapidly passing moments, and will also pass. Living in the light of a terminal diagnosis, I dare to stay conscious of each moment before it is gone. In the same way, I stay conscious of my life even as it passes away.

Life is a small window that opens to us for what seems a blink of an eye, yet, within that window is a plethora of possibilities. We are born into this life to embody spirit and bring love to the world, but we cannot stay indefinitely. This life is temporal, every moment is transient and measured; it is bound by spatial and dimensional limits. We live and love; we create and give; we sow and reap; we sacrifice and die; but try as we may to establish ourselves permanently, we cannot for this is not our land. We are immanent and transcendent beings; we are in the world, but not of the world. (Quezada, Adolfo. *Of Mind and Spirit, 2014).*

Being conscious of my mortality does not mean that I dwell on death. Rather, my focus is on living life to the fullest. But this does not mean that I try to fit everything into the time I have left. It doesn't mean that I try to accomplish all my goals or do all that I have ever wanted to do. Rather, it means that I stay conscious of the moment I am living and appreciate it even as I am living it.

It doesn't matter how many days I have left to live; what matters most is how I am living today. Living life to the fullest does not mean that I add more intensity to it or more activity. It doesn't mean that I fill it with projects and busyness. Sitting on a bench in my back yard watching the sun disappear into the horizon fills my eyes with beauty and my heart with contentment. I will live fully through my dying time.

Having a terminal diagnosis is a daily reminder to me that I am a finite being. My body and mind have done their job and run their course. They will cease to be; but, my soul, which is the essence of my being, will never cease.

Assumptions

Study the assumptions behind your actions. Then study the assumptions behind your assumptions.

Idries Shah

Before the terminal cancer diagnosis, I had assumed that if I ever got a terminal illness my life would be virtually over. Instead, I discovered after my diagnosis that my life was more viable than it had ever been. In fact, it was because of my diagnosis that I gained new impetus for abundant living. In some ways, it was as if my life had just begun, but at a deeper level and with a richer quality.

Before my diagnosis, I assumed that because I had been healthy all my life and had never been admitted to a hospital, I was invulnerable. I assumed that I would never be seriously ill, much less succumb to a terminal illness. I assumed that I would die of old age. So it was surreal to hear from my oncologist that, in fact, I was seriously ill and my illness was incurable. I believed the news intellectually; but, it took a while before I believed it psychically.

It felt strange to admit that I was vulnerable after all. It was hard to accept because, other than my blood test and bone scan, there were no signs of illness. Even now, my apparent good health belies my diagnosis.

My father was a voracious reader. He loved to learn about everything and passed that interest on to his children. When he developed congestive heart failure and received a terminal diagnosis, he kept on reading and acquiring even more knowledge. At the time, I wondered why he wanted to keep learning since he had so little time left to use what he was learning. Now that I have a terminal diagnosis, I can see why he kept on learning. I have realized that what I loved before I was diagnosed, I still love. Consequently, I have continued my own learning. In fact, my appetite for knowledge has increased. My mind has not shut down; my curiosity is still active; and I still crave intellectual stimulation.

I assumed that the diagnosis would compel me to make the ultimate use of the time I had left to live. I thought that I would be compulsive about not wasting even a moment doing nothing. I envisioned my life as an hourglass with precious few grains of sand left to drop. As it turns out, having a terminal diagnosis did not turn me into a timekeeper. Instead, the diagnosis has liberated me from the chains of time. Each moment is still precious to me, but not because there are fewer of them left in my life. Rather, each moment is precious because it is where life itself abides. Living fully and attentively in the moment before me is an experience in timelessness. Life is experience, not hours on the clock.

I assumed that after the diagnosis I would rush to do those things that I had dreamt of doing, but never got around to doing; and to accomplish those things I had intended to do, but never did. I thought of trips taken, adventures experienced, books written, and foreign languages learned. Instead, after the diagnosis, I set aside some dreams that I knew would not be realized; I cancelled my plan to become an accomplished photographer; I decided that in the place of a trip to Italy I would take a trip to New York. I became contented with what I could do instead of striving for what I could not do. To live in the light of a terminal diagnosis means having to adapt to what is and to let go of what isn't.

I assumed that as a result of the diagnosis I would become very religious and follow more strictly the tenets of my religious tradition. I assumed I would be so afraid of dying that I would want something solid and foundational to stand on. Instead, I went the other way. Although I still respected and appreciated the organized religion to which I belonged, the diagnosis gave me the courage to be authentic, and to live according to my basic beliefs without fear of judgment or retribution.

To face a terminal illness requires spirituality grounded in real life. I am not living or dying in the hope of heavenly rewards; rather, my religion is love and love is its own reward. Meanwhile, I live my life one moment at a time. With or without a terminal diagnosis, all that matters is the moment I am living now.

I assumed that the diagnosis would become the focus of my life. I believed that my world would become small and self-contained; like the circling of the wagons when danger approaches. That may actually happen once the symptoms begin to appear. But for now, what I discovered was that the focus of my life is still the welfare of others: my family, my friends, and others who ask for my help. Fortunately, my good health still allows me to visit the physically or emotionally wounded, and to offer them comfort and support. Focus tends to follow interest and my interest is giving of my life, even as it is running out.

I assumed that I would take the diagnosis and retreat indoors and remain there for the duration. Instead, I am drawn outside of my house to interact with nature in all its glory. I seek out nature in every variety, every species, every genre, every ilk, and every shape and color.

I start my day fixated on the early morning moon that greets me, and then guides me on my morning walk with my dog Zorro. In the middle of the day I find myself gazing for long periods into the branches of the giant tree in my back yard for there is where the hummingbirds, the sparrows, the doves, and blackbirds come to serenade my heart. And as night falls and I take Zorro out for one last time before we go to bed, I let my eyes soar to the heavens to drink in the vastness of the universe and the splendor of the stars.

I assumed that the diagnosis would limit my attention to what is going wrong with my body. Instead, my attention is on what is going right in the world. I am aware of the generosity that human beings offer to one another. Sometimes human kindness shows up when and where I least expect to find it.

> *I caught a glimpse of God today. It wasn't in a church or a temple or a mosque. It didn't take the form of heavenly clouds or a majestic sunrise. It was in a common, ordinary, stinky gym.*
>
> *A man with a physical disability was struggling to use the gym equipment when another man stopped his own workout and came to his aid. My heart lifted as I witnessed this act of kindness.*
>
> *The man was totally present to the man with a disability and responded patiently to his needs. He didn't seem to mind that the man he was helping had to do his exercises very slowly. The man helped until he was no longer needed. This bastion of brawn and virility was not the place I expected to find such gentle and compassionate kindness, yet that is where I*

found it. (Quezada. *Of Mind and Spirit, 2014).*

I assumed that my diagnosis would cause me to fear being alone, even for a little while. I thought I would be clinging to those closest to me because eventually I would not be seeing them at all; but I was wrong. Before my diagnosis I needed solitude on a regular basis. I loved people and wanted to spend time with them, yet, if I didn't take time for myself, by myself, I lost my balance. And the same is true after the diagnosis. I realize that my basic needs continue whether I have a terminal diagnosis or not. Today I still have to work hard at balancing my time between being with others and being with myself.

I assumed that the diagnosis would hurry me to leave my mark on the world. I assumed that it would be important for me to leave some kind of legacy by which to be remembered after I die. Since the diagnosis, however, what is important to me is the personal impact I have had on my family and friends. How much I love them and demonstrate that love to them is what matters. How receptive I am of their love for me is also crucial. As I contemplate the end of my life, I am not focused on my legacy; instead, I am living my life as consciously and lovingly as I can, and letting the rest take care of itself. If the footprint of my life helps to guide someone who walks the same path as mine, that is fine.

> *Our goal is not to live in such a way that we will be remembered after our death, but to live our moments fully because we will only live them once. All that will matter is that while we were alive, we loved with our whole heart and lived with our whole being.* (Quezada, Adolfo. *Old Soul, Young Spirit: Reflections on Growing Old, 2015*).

I assumed that the diagnosis would prompt me to go to any lengths to preserve my life, even if for just a while longer. I believed that life was the highest value and that everything should come second to its preservation. I don't believe that now. Today, in the light of the terminal diagnosis, I trust that what is happening in my life needs to be happening. Maybe it's more intuition than trust. In any case, my trust is deeply felt and immutably held. This is why I refuse to wage war against the cancer.

I assumed that I would look upon the diagnosis as an obstacle to overcome instead of a reality to be dealt with. I believed that as long as I took care of myself, all would be well and I could beat back even the terminal cancer. But since the diagnosis, my approach to illness and death has evolved.

I now refuse to look upon the cancer and impending death as a tragedy. The death of my 17-year-old son Roberto was a tragedy; the premature deaths of my three sisters, all in their mid-fifties, were tragedies. But the deaths of my parents, both in their mid-nineties, were not tragedies. At their age, they were natural life events. At my age death will also be a natural life event, a completion of a long and fulfilled life. It will be difficult for me and for my loved ones who will grieve me, but it will not be unfair, unexpected, or unkind.

I assumed that I would be quick to give purpose to the diagnosis. I believed that without a purpose my death would be in vain. I believe now, however, that neither terminal illness nor death needs to be justified in order to be accepted. Both illness and death are natural life events, and they happen whether we assign them a purpose or not. Life has its own purpose; death has its own purpose; and I accept each for its own sake.

What I assumed prior to the diagnosis has definitely evolved. Perhaps it will evolve even more as I experience the cancer and move closer to death. Evolution is a sign of growth, and growth is a sign of life. I hope to continue evolving every day of my life.

Gratitude

Cultivate the habit of being grateful for every good thing that comes to you, and to give thanks continuously. And because all things have contributed to your advancement, you should include all things in your gratitude.

Ralph Waldo Emerson

Even before the cancer begins its more aggressive course within me, I am already grateful for much that has come and is to come.

I am aware that my illness is incurable. I know that the probable symptoms of cancer are debilitating, painful, and progressive. I anticipate a very difficult time ahead. But that should be enough. I don't have to add negative thoughts and emotions to it. Hopefully, my faith will mitigate the stress, confusion, fear, and anger that will probably come.

I have no choice but to accept the diagnosis that has been given to me and to deal with it, but I do have a choice as to *how* I will deal with it. I cannot control the circumstances, but I can surely control how I respond to them.

My emotions emanate from my thoughts. They are the result of what I tell myself. I don't have to allow depression and hopelessness to bring me down. I don't have to assume helplessness or condemn myself to isolation.

I will not be a victim of cancer; instead, I will actively partner with it as it takes me where I need to go. I will manage it to the best of my ability to avoid inordinate and unnecessary pain and suffering; and I will honor and respect it as an integral part of my life and death.

A healthy response to the diagnosis does not necessitate a Pollyanna attitude or a state of denial. On the contrary, it is crucial that I remain conscious of the reality before me and allow a sense of equanimity in my response. For example, I owe it to myself to avoid pain and suffering, but not at any cost. I owe it to myself to avoid death, but not at any cost.

I need to respond to the diagnosis emotionally *and* spiritually. My emotions come and go; but my spirit, while grounded in my humanity, soars beyond my worldly concerns.

I have no death wish. I want to be alive for my family for as long as I can be. At the same time, staying alive at any cost and by whatever means necessary is incongruent with my belief in the natural flow of life and death. This is not resignation on my part, but simply the acceptance of the laws of nature without struggle or resistance, without grievance or appeal.

Responding to death's call is actually life-giving to me. But let me be clear. Although death may lead to the ultimate liberation of my soul, I would still choose life within the confines of my humanity if that path were open to me. I would still prefer to remain among my fellow human beings, loving and serving one another. I acquiesce to death only because it is already on my front porch with one foot in the door.

I face imminent death not as a warrior ready to do battle with it, but as one prepared to surrender to life and all that comes with life, including death. My courage comes, not from personal bravado, but from the grace of God. I am not afraid of annihilation because when I cease to be, God will still be. I believe that God is life, and life never ceases.

Cancer has decided to visit me. I can bar the door against it; I can pretend that I'm not home; I can even run away from it to some deserted land. But they tell me the cancer is already within me; it is already consuming my healthy cells. So I have decided to welcome it into my life and to treat it with respect. I don't ask "Why me?" I don't pray that this cup pass me by. I just acknowledge, "Oh, it's my turn."

There was a period of time when I became very fatalistic, and adopted an attitude of futility regarding my body. I stopped going to the gym and started eating carbs compulsively. I told myself that it didn't matter what happened to my body since it was going to disintegrate eventually anyway. This approach did not serve me well and I soon began to experience the logical consequences of such behavior. I realized that although I was accepting the diagnosis intellectually, I had unconsciously disowned my body prematurely. My body was still very much a part of who I was, yet I was virtually abandoning it. I was leaving it unprotected, unattended, and unloved.

To love God is to love myself, and to love myself is to love my whole self, including my body, diseased or not. My body needs my protection, my attention, and my love up until the moment of my death.

By truly accepting the cancer, I am also accepting my body, regardless of its infirmity, its deterioration, and the pain and suffering it must eventually endure. My body has served me well for 75 years and deserves my gratitude and my appreciation. In light of this revelation my intent is to be as healthy as I can be, even through the process of dying. I will not leave this body physically or emotionally until it no longer needs me.

The cancer that grows within me is part of my body now, so to love my body is to love the cancer too. If I reject any part of myself, including the "bad" cells that kill off the "good" cells, I am rejecting my whole self.

It may seem strange to love the illness that is slowly killing me, yet I do love it. Cancer is not good or bad, it is neutral. It is in its nature to kill off red cells. That's what it was designed to do. I don't blame the cancer for doing its job. I don't blame anything or anyone. I respect it for its steady course and determined mission. I accept it as a part of me and a part of my life and death.

A diagnosis of incurable cancer is not usually something to accept with gratitude, but in my case it is, because this type of cancer literally gives me a grace period. That is, a time up front for plenty of joyful living and an opportunity to bring closure to my life.

I am grateful for the extended time I have been granted to gather the forces of my better self, hold tightly to those whom I love, and smell the orange blossoms to my heart's content. I am grateful for the time I've been given to close out my life gradually and consciously. I am grateful for this prelude to the ominous storm that looms in the not too distant future.

I am grateful to the cancer for offering itself to me as the catalyst for the eventual disintegration of my body and my ultimate annihilation into God. I am grateful to the doctors and nurses and other medical personnel who will use their personal and professional skills to get me through this inevitable ordeal. I am grateful for the medications that will help manage my disease and minimize my pain. I am grateful to those who will keep me in their heart when things get really tough.

As I live in the light of a terminal diagnosis, I experience anticipatory grief for what I will lose. As the cancer continues to invade my body, it will take away those capabilities on which I have depended. I grieve the future loss of my energy and the activities, even the simple ones, in which I love participating. I grieve the good health that I enjoy today. I grieve the freedom from pain and my clearheadedness that I have now. I grieve my independence from prescription drugs, and my flexibility to come and go as I do now. I grieve the ability I have to help others, and my own self-sufficiency. I grieve being treated as a normal, healthy person, and participating in the world as such. I grieve my future. I grieve the dreams I have of what could be and my plans for great adventure; and I grieve my long-term goals and expectations. All of this anticipatory grieving is necessary and appropriate. Yet, even as I allow my heart to break with grief for all that I will lose, I also allow my heart to fill with gratitude for first having had all that I will lose.

I am grateful for the gift of life itself, the grace of being. I am grateful for the time I've been allotted on this paradise called Earth. In that time I have been blessed with a life partner to love and by whom to be loved. My life has been good mainly because of her. I am grateful for my four children who are the fruit of God's love and the reason for my joy. To add joy upon joy, I am blessed with five beautiful, loving, precious grandchildren. They are the proof to me that life and love will carry on beyond my time.

I am grateful for the good health I have enjoyed my whole life, and even now. Sometimes I took my health for granted, but mostly, I have been aware of the gift of health and I have used it as the foundation from which to serve others, including the terminally ill. I am grateful for the extra physical and mental energy that I have received through the years. It has enabled me not only to conceive of ways to be of service to others, but also to carry out those ways

I am grateful for the men and women who have graced my life with their presence, their support, their compassion, and their true friendship. They helped me to become a better friend.

I am grateful for the opportunities that were open to me at all the stages of my life. It seemed as if one opportunity led to another and then another. I am grateful for all those persons for whom I have had the pleasure to work. Some were more difficult to work for than others, but I learned life lessons from them all.

I am grateful for my family of origin who gave me a foundation from which to grow into adulthood. My parents did the best they could and my siblings were always supportive and continue to be so even now. I am grateful for all that I will lose because it once was mine to have.

> *Gratitude is our natural way of being in the world; it is our positive outlook that is open and inviting to whatever comes; it is a readiness of spirit that is prepared to make the best of what comes in life; including joy and suffering, illness and heath, life and death.* (Quezada. *Of Mind and Spirit, 2014).*

Choices

One's philosophy is not best expressed in words; it is expressed in the choices one makes...and the choices we make are ultimately our responsibility.

Eleanor Roosevelt

As the cancer progresses I will be faced with a choice between two alternatives: I can resist what is coming my way or I can surrender to it. I can fight against what is or I can be open and receptive to it.

I make choices. Rather than treat the various symptoms that come with WM as indications that something is wrong with my body, I choose to accept each one of them as a part of my dying process. Whether it is my heart getting weaker because it has to work harder to pump my thickened blood through my veins, my eyes beginning to blur, my lymph nodes being invaded by tumors, my mind becoming confused or other symptoms; I choose to look upon these symptoms as merely part of the natural course of my dying.

Although I feel relieved because the cancer is growing slowly, I am also aware, at an unconscious level, that I still have the sword of Damocles menacingly poised over my head. Sometimes I am afraid of what might happen when the cancer symptoms begin to manifest, but then my heart chooses gratitude over fear.

Already the protein in my bone marrow is elevated and the blood in my veins has to be monitored for viscosity. But all of this is still manageable at this point. I am still able to enjoy a pain-free existence and a clear head to read, write, and communicate with friends and family. But even as I take pleasure in all aspects of my life, I am acutely aware of my friends whose cancer symptoms have already engulfed their lives. I don't know how they do it. May I have the strength and courage to emulate them.

I know that my oncologist is well trained and has years of experience treating cancer. I am especially fortunate to have an oncologist who is well acquainted with my rare type of cancer. I trusted him to diagnose me accurately and he did. He has a wonderful reputation in his field and has co-authored research with the top oncologists in the country. I trust him implicitly, yet, when it comes to my life, I choose to trust myself above all. I trust my intuition, and I trust the guidance that comes from within. I will have a choice between following the treatment recommendations of my oncologist and following my own instincts. Because it is my life, my choice will be personal and congruent with what I believe.

This may sound presumptuous. After all, the oncologist is the professional; he has all the training; he understands WM better than most, and certainly better than I do. Yet, I am the expert on myself. I am the only one who knows what I am willing to do to extend my life, and what I am not. Only I know exactly how I prefer to live and die.

My healthy cells are already being killed off by my aggressive, unhealthy cells; my sense of it is that I don't need to add to the killing through chemotherapy and other drugs. My immune system has already been compromised by the cancer; I don't need to shut it down with drugs.

For me, the number of days that I live is not as important as the quality of those days. I have embarked on the river of illness, and I trust it to carry me to the ocean of death.

Pain may eventually engulf my body. I won't welcome it. I will want it gone. But if it is to stay, let it make me more sensitive than I am. Fear may overwhelm my heart when I become symptomatic. And if fear comes, let it evoke the courage within me. Let it strengthen my resolve.

Sometimes, when our illness has wracked our body with excruciating pain and we are feeling so nauseous that we would welcome death, we are not concerned about the state of our soul. When our heart is in despair and our mind is clouded and confused, all we care about is getting through the next moment. Nothing matters more to us than to end the agony. In the midst of the pain we feel so powerless that we can't even call upon our spiritual resources for help. My friend Joni says that at times like these the spirit within prays for us. She says, "It is a prayer that comes from the deepest deep..." (Quezada, Adolfo. *Transcending Illness through the Power of Belief, 2011).*

It sounds glib in the abstract to refer to pain as part of the process of becoming whole, because when the pain actually comes it will be harder for me to be so philosophical about it. I will choose to relieve pain pharmaceutically as long as the side effects of the drug are not worse than the pain. But sometimes, even with medication, the pain is inexorable. I will choose to avoid unnecessary pain whenever it is possible and prudent to do so.

Pain, like suffering in general, should not be sought after or permitted because of any perceived intrinsic value. It is only when pain is inevitable, that I choose to assign purpose and meaning to it. Only when there is no other path, do I choose to enter into the pain and allow it to transform me.

It is not difficult to be present to life when I am not feeling pain or discomfort; but whether I will be able to stay conscious of my present moments, when they are filled with the agony of a cancer-riddled body, remains to be seen.

As I enter into the pain of the cancer, I will come face to face with my authentic self. Pain has a way of exposing authenticity. Being authentic, that is, dropping away the masks I sometimes wear in order to be accepted or to protect myself, will make it impossible for me to pretend that I am someone I am not. When I am hurting, the pain will be my focus.

I used to weep for those who were dying because I believed that dying was the ultimate suffering. But I have realized that it is for those who have no choice but to continue living and suffering with chronic illness and severe physical or emotional pain that I should be weeping. Those of us who are close to death will soon be at peace, but those who must continue to suffer life at its worst, day in and day out, deserve my tears and compassion. It will be easier for me to accept death at the end of my illness than it will be to accept my illness. Perhaps it is because the effects of my illness have only just begun, but more likely it is because it is easier to die of a chronic illness than it is to live with a chronic illness.

Through my fear and trepidation I will choose to be with my illness, to listen to its voice, and to learn its lessons well.

The illness that has brought me down now lifts me to a higher place. Courage carries me forth and faith sustains me. I am not alone. In the midst of my infirmity the blessings come. My mind opens so that I may learn the lessons of my illness. My heart expands to receive the love that is born of my surrender. My flesh acquiesces to the demands of my condition. My bones may be broken and my blood spilled, yet my core is pure and my soul is whole. (Quezada. *Transcending Illness through the Power of Belief, 2011*).

Even as I embrace the impermanence of my existence as a human being, I choose to believe in the permanence of my being in God. Dying, especially when it comes slowly, is a profound spiritual experience. It is transformational, transitional, and transcendental.

The diagnosis has made me aware that I am in need of healing, but the healing I require is not physical; rather, it is spiritual. My soul is in need of rest and restoration. It has journeyed far and seeks a place of respite and repose. My age and my illness have already begun to limit my doing, but nothing can take away my capacity for being.

My dying time is filled with deep appreciation for precious living. Even before I die, I am already choosing to release my hold on my separate self, and beginning to dissolve into oneness with all that is. My finite being is carried forth by infinite love. Just the awareness of my imminent death quiets my spirit, opens my mind to a consciousness beyond my immediate personal self, and expands the purview of my soul.

The morning hours are precious to me now. They have always been a time of stillness and serenity, a time to be alone with God. But now they take on even more significance. Although God is within me every hour of the day as I work and play, walk my dog in the desert, or visit with my friends and family; the morning hours are the time of sweet surrender into the essence of God. This is the time my body rests, my mind empties, and my spirit soars toward the ultimate dimension of being. I don't know exactly what will happen to my soul when I die. I do know that this morning I am within God and God is within me.

When something comes my way that provokes anxiety, I stop and pay attention to my breath. I don't know why anxiety and breathing consciously from the belly are mutually exclusive, but they are. It is as if my breath blows away my fear of the unknown.

I find that praying and meditating is not just something that I should do, or something that is good to do. Rather, it is something that I must do if I want to stay afloat. It is my lifeline and I dare not let it go. Meditation mimics dying. In both cases my false self falls away, leaving only my essential self.

I don't look for signs or miracles beyond what has already been revealed to me. My breath is the sign of life, and the love I have given and received is the greatest miracle of all.

As I contemplate my death, less and less matters to me, but what does matter, matters a lot. Love matters, authenticity matters, the welfare of my loved ones matters, the beauty of nature matters, the condition of our human family matters, forgiveness matters, and remembering my oneness with God matters.

My priorities have changed dramatically. I seem to have less patience for the superfluous. I prefer to watch a hummingbird at my window to watching a senseless, violent, plotless show on television. I would rather connect with a friend than to write about friendship. I drop whatever project I am working on to respond to my dog Zorro when he wants to play. In short, living consciously has become much more important to me than accomplishing projects.

On the day the diagnosis of incurable cancer was confirmed I stopped imagining the future. I knew I had an immediate future to consider, but the long-range future that had concerned me before was now an empty canvass that would remain empty. It was not a traumatic realization; it merely brought my focus to the present moment where it has remained.

Fulfillment

*Do not seek death. Death will find
you. But seek the road which makes death
a fulfillment.*

Dag Hammarskjold

As I approach the end of my life, I am fulfilled from the long and fruitful journey I have taken.

I have been happily married for more than five decades, and I fathered four wonderful human beings, who in turn have parented five precious souls. I worked hard in various capacities and accomplished many of my personal goals. In other words, the potential of my life on earth has, for the most part, been realized.

Of course, when I die my presence will be missed by my loved ones and my absence will be grieved. This is natural and necessary. But I hope that no one will think that I got a raw deal or that I was treated unfairly by life. I do not feel cheated. On the contrary, I was blessed with a lifetime of love given and love received. I was blessed with wonderful opportunities and with the good health to take advantage of them. I was blessed with a God-filled soul that has carried me through my life and will carry me into my death.

I have had my share of tragedy and discontent, yet, I am a fortunate man. I have regrets about roads not taken and about some that I took, but mostly, my life has been filled with wonderful opportunities and life-enhancing experiences. My latter years especially have been graced with profound contentment.

To fulfill means to complete, to finish, and to terminate. These words certainly describe my end of life. But to fulfill also means to satisfy, to realize, and to arrive at full potential. These words describe my life even better.

Yes, there is a completion at the end of life; there is a finish, an ending, a termination. My end of life, however, includes so much more than a conclusion. It has to do with the realization of many dreams, with the satisfaction of how my life turned out, and with knowing that; although I fell short on many measures, God brought me to my full human potential in spite of myself.

Above all else, my communion with God is the fulfillment of my life purpose. There is nothing in my life that has fulfilled me as completely as surrendering myself to the God of my soul, and allowing the spirit of God to live and love through me. They say that dying is something we do alone, but, come what may, I am not alone.

The fulfillment that comes from communing with God includes sharing God's spirit with those who share this world with me. Sharing God does not mean talking about God or even writing about God. It means being the essence of God to others. It means loving others with God's love and serving others with God's energy. It means encouraging others to fulfill their full potential too.

Ever since I can remember I have wanted to be of service to others, especially those who were suffering in any way. In light of my passionate desire to alleviate suffering in the world, it made sense that I wanted very badly to join the Peace Corps when I graduated from college. Unfortunately, for several reasons, that never happened. For most of my life I lamented that road not taken. Fortunately, some of the roads that I did take on my life journey allowed me to fulfill my desire to be of service to others.

Besides several detours that included stints in politics, state and national government, banking, journalism, and education; I also held jobs in which I was able to fulfill my passion for helping others. I quit a career in banking in order to take a job as a youth director for the YMCA in the African American community of San Diego. That experience stretched me to grow as an individual and as a member of the human family.

On another occasion I quit my job as a staff writer for a major newspaper in order to found a nonprofit organization that helps the poor. That organization is still going strongly today. I returned to the newspaper, but in my spare time I founded a church-based program through which families with means befriended families with limited means. Although there was financial help available as well as material assistance, the strongest part of the program was the family-to-family connection. So, in a sense, between those two organizations, I had designed my own Peace Corps.

The best career move I ever made was to leave a secure job as an assistant dean at the University of Arizona and return to school to train as a counselor. For more than 25 years I practiced counseling and psychotherapy. Here was another opportunity to help men and women who were hurting emotionally and spiritually. I dealt with wounded psyches, broken hearts, lost souls, and those trying to overcome the damage done to them through childhood abuse.

The work was difficult and fulfilling; painful and healing. I have retired from the professional practice, but not from the personal practice of helping others overcome the hardships of life.

Counseling entails a lot of listening, but it also includes words. Sometimes a word or two can make all the difference in the world for someone who wants so much to be understood. I have used words to affirm others, but also to encourage, challenge, guide, and inspire them. Words have also been my tool of choice for helping others through the books I write. One fulfilling experience that I have often is when someone tells me that they have been helped by something I wrote. Sometimes they tell me that they feel as if I wrote the words especially and specifically for them. In a sense, I did.

This is my eighteenth book. I usually write about what I need to learn. The research, the pondering, the creative process, and the actual writing are all life-giving to me. I am grateful for the seed of spiritual sustenance that was sown in my heart, and for the ability to bring it to fruition through the written word.

I have come to love my life more than ever. In fact, these last few years have been the best of all. It follows that I don't want my life to end. But it is also true that what takes form must also disintegrate. I know that death is an integral part of life, and that if I accept life I must also accept death.

Like the leaves falling from a tree in autumn, my plans and schemes are dropping away. How strange it is to bring to mind something I have been looking forward to doing, then to suddenly realize that although the spirit is still there and willing, the time is no longer there. And so I set aside some dreams, not with sadness, but with gentle understanding; not with resignation, but with acceptance of what is, and the patience to wait for what must be.

Waiting. That is the initial treatment plan for asymptomatic WM. Plain and simple – wait and watch. That's it. No drugs, no surgeries, no infusions, just waiting.

It seems counterintuitive to wait for cancer symptoms to become aggressive and life-threatening before addressing them, yet that is what the research has concluded is the best approach for the treatment of asymptomatic WM.

My oncologist told me it could take years for the serious cancer symptoms to appear. But it really depends on how long the cancer has already been growing in my body. A woman who was diagnosed with WM wrote a book about her experience. She was told by her doctors not to worry about the symptoms since they would not manifest for years. Unfortunately, four weeks later she had to begin treatment to address WM symptoms.

And so I wait, perhaps for an extended time, perhaps not. It is hard to wait; yet, waiting has been so much a part of my life. From the moment of conception to the present, I have been waiting. I waited to be born, I waited to be cared for, I waited to grow up, I waited to get a job, I waited to retire, and now I am waiting to get really sick and die.

Waiting requires patience and patience requires faith. French philosopher Simone Weil wrote that, "Waiting patiently in expectation is the foundation of the spiritual life." But does waiting in faith mean that if I believe strongly enough and I wait long enough I will eventually get what I expect? I don't believe so. Instead, I believe that waiting faithfully means waiting with open-ended expectation. Of course I have my personal preferences, but I wait, believing that whatever life presents to me I will accept and make the most of it.

Mythologist Joseph Campbell wrote that, "We must let go of the life we've planned, so as to accept the one that is waiting for us." I learned that one the hard way. Let me explain.

I quit a good job because I believed that there was something better suited for me out there somewhere. When time passed and I had not found work, I began to despair. One day I was home alone, sitting on the floor with my head in my hands, feeling discouraged and impatient. Internally, I was asking the universe what was to become of me. Suddenly, I heard words definitely addressed to me. They were disembodied, but they were clear and direct: "Wait for what must be!" I was puzzled, but not afraid. I didn't know the meaning of these words then, but later I did.

Within weeks my son Roberto was struck by a car and died two days later. Obviously, my whole life changed dramatically. I was fortunate not to have a job so that I could attend to my family during this time of tragic loss.

Eventually, my life took a different direction, one that I had not anticipated. Personally and professionally what came was not at all what I had expected. I ended up going back to school to retrain for a profession that fulfilled me beyond my wildest imagination. I had suffered greatly from the loss of my son, and now I had the opportunity to help others who were suffering in the same way.

My waiting is different now; I no longer wait for anything in particular. Instead, I wait for what must be.

I said to my soul, be still and wait
without hope, for hope would be hope for
the wrong thing; wait without love, for love
would be love for the wrong thing; there is

yet faith, but the faith and the love are all in the waiting. Wait without thought, for you are not ready for thought: so the darkness shall be the light, and the stillness the dancing.

T.S. Eliot

I have never been much of a procrastinator, but now there is a good reason to get done what needs to be done. Because I know my time is limited, I operate under the belief that if I don't do something now, it probably won't ever get done. This book falls into that category. I figure that if I don't complete it while I still have the capacity to do so, the effects of the cancer will prevent it from ever seeing the light of day.

Usually, cancer patients suffer from their infirmity for a while and then, with treatment and good fortune, they go into remission. Of course, they are very grateful for the reprieve. I feel the same way, except that in my case I have not yet experienced the serious cancer symptoms because my cancer has a slow progression. So the way I see it, my "remission" has come first, and then the cancer will set in with a vengeance. Of course I am very grateful for the calm before the storm.

A time-limited life seems to be in stark contrast to a fulfilled life, yet, in my experience they are complementary. My awareness of my imminent death prompts me to settle for nothing less than a fulfilled life; conversely, a fulfilled life has nothing to do with quantity and everything to do with quality.

I will die to this world only once, and I intend to give my undivided attention to my dying time. I am aware of what is happening all around me, but especially of what is happening within me.

> *Awareness of our mortality radically enlivens us and prompts us to live each moment of our life deliberately.* (Quezada. *Transcending Illness through the Power of Belief, 2011).*

I am definitely aware of my mortality, but I am also gratefully aware of my aliveness, and of all the dimensions of the heart that come with being alive. Fear and courage are not mutually exclusive, nor are life and death. At times I face illness and death with fear and anxiety, but also with courage and resolve. I cannot talk myself into courage. Logical reasoning is a function of my mind, while courage emanates from my heart, the core of my being where God abides.

I am living my life even as it slips away from me. I am dying even as I experience new life. Conscious of my mortality, I cannot afford to float through life half-conscious of what I am doing. My true being insists that I live authentically, responsibly, and purposefully.

My courage emanates from my heart because my heart is filled with love of family, love of God, and love of life. I can be courageous because my wife Judy and my children Maria, Cristina, and Miguel stand by me no matter what I am facing. My heart breaks for anyone who has to face life and death issues without the love and support of their family. The welfare of my family has given purpose to my life, and now, as I walk the treacherous path of cancer, I am afraid, yet courageous, because my loved ones have my back. I can be courageous because I am anchored in the love of God. Only love can give me the courage to live, and only love can give me the courage to die.

Even in the midst of our temporal life, there is the constancy of love. We live and die, but no matter the length of our life, and whatever its magnitude, it makes an imprint on those whom we love. We live not for ourselves alone, but also for those whose seeds we carry and those whose lives we touch. We are more than time and space, and the impact we have on one another transcends the boundaries of our birth and death. (Quezada. *Old Soul, Young Spirit: Reflections on Growing Old, 2015*).

Living

A woman has to live her life, or live to repent not having lived it.

D.H. Lawrence

I learned about living from those who were dying.

In my past writings about purposeful living and conscious dying, I have included my friend Alejandra. I looked to her to teach me how to die, but instead she taught me how to live. This is my story about Alejandra.

Giving purpose to our terminal illness may sound grandiose and global, but purpose need not necessarily apply beyond our immediate circle of life.

Once I befriended a young woman named Alejandra. I got to know her well at several spiritual retreats. She was a peaceful person with a beautiful smile. A single mother of two small children, she had not had an easy time of it. In fact, she had experienced much emotional and physical pain in her twenty four years of life. It was hard to tell from her demeanor that she was dying of bone cancer. Only her amputated leg and bulging tumors gave it away. Her husband had left her, and her illness limited the time she could spend with her children. Her world was coming to an end, yet there was such peace in her face, a peace I did not understand. I visited her regularly over a period of months, including her last days in a hospice setting. I wanted to be supportive of her in every way I could.

One day, not long before Alejandra died, I began asking her probing questions about her philosophy of life and death. I asked her what things she would want to tell the world if she could. I even asked her what she would do if she were granted health and more time to live. As to the profound message she would issue from her deathbed – she had none. She said, however, that she wanted to write a few words to her son and daughter. She already had written a poem of love to her mother. I began to see that Alejandra's scope of life was in the here and now. Her attention was on the immediate, the local, and the real.

To my question about a second chance at life, Alejandra told me she would not change much if she were to stay alive and get well. She had no plans greater than to go to the park with her children and watch them at play. She said she would want to work and to go for a ride once in a while. She said she wanted to do the "ordinary things of life," and to live one moment at a time, enjoying it fully, just being. She spoke of simple things, of the present time, and of littleness. She seemed to be saying, "I will just smell this flower one more time before I go."

Alejandra's body succumbed to the cancer and she died soon thereafter, yet she was one of the healthiest persons I have ever known. Her wholesomeness ran deeper than the killer tumors, and her love transcended any illusions of time and space.

Alejandra was buried in a potter's field as anonymously as she had lived. But I had known her, and I will always remember her. (Quezada. *Transcending Illness through the Power of Belief, 2011).*

A few days before Alejandra died she recited for me a few words from her favorite poem:

I see at the end of my rough road
that I was the architect of my own destiny.
I loved, I was loved, the sun caressed my
face.

Life, you owe me nothing! Life, we
are at peace.

Amado Nervo

Today, in the light of my terminal diagnosis, I ask myself the same questions that I asked Alejandra. Only, in my case, I actually *have* been granted more time to live in relatively good health. Time appears to be on my side. Because I have an indolent cancer, that is, slow moving and essentially asymptomatic, I am being granted an extension of time well beyond the date of the diagnosis.

To the question of what I would do with more time, I would say that I am living out my answer. I am being and doing what Alejandra would have wanted to be and do. I am being my basic self with no pretences or facades. I am being God's love in the world. I am doing simple, ordinary things; living consciously and fully; and joyfully experiencing the natural world that is pure gift.

As I awaken to the light of each new day, I celebrate the gift of another chance, another go at life.

Now I am at the threshold of a new adventure. I embark on a journey into dark and unchartered waters. I move toward the challenge of the day, believing that I have been given what I need to meet it.

***

My friend Tony was 18 years old. He was dying of cancer. One of his legs had been amputated, but he hobbled around the best he could. It's hard to keep a good young man down. This was about the time that Elizabeth Kubler-Ross' research on death and dying was just becoming known. Her work helped bring the subject of death out into the open and challenged society's denial of it. It was helpful research, but even good information can be misused.

Several women who were helping Tony's family had been reading about Kubler-Ross' stages of dying and they were determined to apply them to Tony. Tony, however, was not about dying; he wanted to focus on life and said so clearly. He still wanted to experience a world he hardly knew. He was also discovering his own spirituality in the process. But the women insisted. They claimed that Tony was in denial and must face up to the reality that he was dying. They actually became confrontive with him and his mother about it. For them,

Tony's focus on living was tantamount to the denial of his imminent death. Fortunately, Tony and his mother told the two women to stay away.

To revere life and to want to relish every precious moment of it did not mean that Tony was in denial of death. Conversely, his acceptance of death did not mean that he didn't want to live until his last breath. Tony's awareness of his imminent death did not negate his lust for life.

Tony told me that he wanted to have time to live a different life than he had been living, one that would reflect God. He said he wanted to go on living even with only one leg. The wholeness he sought was not for his body alone. Even as he prayed for his recovery, he asked me, "But why is it we only ask for recovery? Shouldn't we be asking that God's will be done whatever that may be?"

I helped dig Tony's grave and buried him on the grounds of his favorite place in the whole world, a Benedictine monastery in Southern Arizona where he had attended several retreats. I remember Tony. I remember his deep faith and his zest for life, even in the face of death. I learned from Tony that even when we are actively dying, life wants to be fully lived.

***

My sister Mary Helen was dying of cancer. She and I talked about time-bound matters like being able to be with her children and grandchildren, and about timeless matters like faith and love. She told me of her wishes and regrets, and about her fear and gratitude.

Mary Helen was a holy woman and I was privileged to accompany her to the edge of life. I remember thinking at the time of her death that death does not discriminate; it comes to good people as well as bad.

***

I had some quality time with my sister Alicia in the months before she died of cancer. We listened to music and we laughed a lot. When my son was killed some years before, Alicia wrote me, "This morning it didn't make sense that the sun was shining and the birds were singing. I don't think they know. Who does one tell about a broken heart?" I felt the same way after her death.

***

Less than two years after Alicia's death, my father died. I was with him a lot in the last months of his life. I interpreted some of his dreams and we talked about what he believed about life and death. He was not afraid of death, but he was afraid to die unforgiven of his iniquities. He didn't believe that God had forgiven him for the mistakes he had made in life. I remember the anguish in his eyes when he asked me whether God would forgive him. All of my assurances that he was indeed forgiven by God fell on deaf ears. He continued to fear what might happen to his soul.

I wish my father would have believed me when I told him that he was dying with no debts and that he was entering the next phase of his life completely cleansed. Better still, I wish someone would have helped him to experience the power of forgiveness many years before so that he might have been able to anticipate death more peacefully.

I sat up with my father through his last night. It was a long and arduous night for him. He asked me repeatedly how much longer he had to wait to die. At dawn he seemed more peaceful; and with the morning light came his ultimate release.

***

My mother died of Alzheimer's disease six years ago. Her death brought to a close nearly a century of zestful living. I sat by her bed the night she died. It was incredulous to me that this woman who had been in perpetual motion all her life was now so woefully still. How could I say goodbye to the woman who had given me life and raised me into adulthood? How could I reconcile myself to the reality that the vibrancy and strength that had influenced my life so much was now gone? Only a week had passed since my mother had taken my hand and held it to her face for a long time. Although she could no longer speak, her loving gesture said so much to me. She must have known at some level that the end of her life was near.

My mother, who was 95 years old, did not want to die. She had made that perfectly clear. She would say, "We all have to die sometime." Then she would quickly add, "But not just yet." Life was exciting for her and she simply did not see the point of dying. As I remained with my mother's lifeless body I thought back to the times of silent companionship that she and I had shared. One day she and I sat silently under the shade of two large orange trees watching the black ravens frolic on the green lawn of the nursing home where she had lived for several years. As we sat there drinking in the beauty of that fresh summer morning I pondered the nature of being. I wondered to myself whether my mother was really living now. I wondered what, if anything, she might be thinking. I questioned whether sitting for hour after hour in a wheelchair staring into space or sleeping off the last dosage of medication constituted life. A dynamic, spirited woman, who raised seven children and preserved a marriage for more than six decades until she was widowed, now appeared to be just existing, but not really living. I wondered if there was more to her life now than just waiting to die. Then it dawned on me: she was responding to life from who she was and what she had at the moment.

I concluded that life comes in all colors, breadths, and depths. It cannot be evaluated according to anyone's expectations. Life is precious in the eyes of God from our first breath to our last, regardless of its quality. Life is miraculous and does not need to justify itself. Life is life and, whether hardy or faint, it must be cherished for its own sake.

Surrender

In the process of dying, the concept of surrender, at first, is completely entangled with the concepts and accompanying feelings of hope and despair and giving up and fighting and pleading and denying. When the heart sighs and begins its surrender to suffering, hell dissolves before our eyes.

                    Stephen Levine

I will not give in to cancer, even when its symptoms bring me low.

I will not be like a gazelle, locked in the jaws of a lion, with no recourse but to accept its fate. I will not be vanquished by the power of a disease. Yet, I am prepared to surrender wholeheartedly to a power greater than cancer, greater than life or death.

Surrender is not the same as resignation; rather, it is the awareness of what is, and the determination to make the best of it. I do not surrender to the cancer as to a formidable opponent, but rather, as a fact of life that cannot be denied, but can be used for good.

Is there a difference between "giving in" and surrendering? There is to me. If I give in, I cease resisting because it is futile to continue the fight against the killer cells and the other cancer symptoms. It means that I take on the role of victim and assume my powerlessness. But if I surrender, I enter into the experience of pain, suffering and death with my whole being. Rather than be taken into the jaws of the lion without recourse, I feed the lion with my body, I nourish it, and I become the lion.

What is the meaning of *surrender?* The dictionary definition of *surrender* is to give up, as, into the power of another. The *sur* in *surrender* means "over," "above," "in addition." *Render* means "to cease to be; to give." In other words, to surrender is to give myself up to a force greater than myself. For me, God is that force.

The prelude to death demands of me a radical surrender. It asks me to let go of anything that separates me from God. Love compels surrender.

In the desert of life we reach the point of full surrender. Here in the poverty of the soul, we release our hold on the ephemeral and embrace the eternal. (Adolfo Quezada, *Walking with God: Reflections on Life's Meaning,* Liguori, MO., Liguori Publications, 1990).

I surrender, but surrender does not mean that I resign myself to my fate. It does not mean that I give up in defeat or that I relinquish hope. To surrender in the prelude to death means that I set aside my usual defenses; that I release my grip on control; and that I accept what is. It means that my efforts are no longer directed at fighting what seems inevitable, but instead, are focused on evoking the strength, courage, and perseverance from within that are needed for me to get through the final chapter of my life.

In surrender, I do not become a prisoner of an overpowering force, rather, I move beyond my egocentric self toward union with God. In surrender, I make myself available to the divine will; I yield to divine intelligence; and I listen to the wisdom that emanates from the depths of my soul.

> *In this ultimate surrender, we move beyond our self, toward union with God. We open our self to the power of love and the hope of possibility.* (Adolfo Quezada. *Radical Love.* New York: Paulist Press, 2010).

In the prelude to death I am left impotent. I am confronted with the reality of my humanity, including my vulnerability, my dependency, my fragility, and my finitude. Throughout my life, I have protected myself with power, yet I am now asked by life to let go of all my defenses and to acknowledge that the only real power is the power of love.

In surrender, I stop resisting the terminal illness that looms over my future. Instead, I join forces with it. Surrendering will not leave me powerless. On the contrary, it will endow me with the power of that to which I surrender.

This is not suicidal ideation, but rather, self-deliverance into the natural course of life and death. Rather than be a victim of my terminal illness, I partner with it in the dance of death; I participate actively in the whole experience; and I own my illness as well as my death.

Surrender radically transforms my life. No longer do I cling to the superfluous. Naked and guileless, I commend my temporal self to the Ground of Being.

When I surrender, the possibility of transformation is born. As I release my hold on the worldly and inessential, I move beyond my limited self and into the state of spiritual awareness.

I do not surrender to cancer because cancer is finite like I am. Cancer has a beginning, middle, and end. This is true of my life on earth as well. Cancer is limited, as am I. Instead, I surrender to that which is infinite, which has no boundaries, which has always been and will always be.

When I first heard the terminal cancer diagnosis from my oncologist, my first thought was, "Okay, I guess it's time to turn in the equipment that I borrowed." As the news sunk in, I remembered how attached I had become to "the equipment." After all, my body has seen me through a lot in the last seven and a half decades. I know that even now I am not as in touch with my body as I should be, but nevertheless, it is near and dear to me.

In the months since receiving the diagnosis, I have come to appreciate and care for my body more than ever before. Of course, I dread the time when my body will begin to break down as the cancer invades me from within. I may quip about returning "the equipment," yet, I am soberly aware that it will not be that easy to do.

Of course, my preference is to keep all pain and suffering at bay in the process of dying. I prefer a peaceful death - an Easter Sunday without a Good Friday. I am afraid of having to live through an extended period of physical agony, and worse, the loss of functionality.

Surrendering my physical self is not something that I do once and for all. Rather, it is something I will need to do over and over as I experience the full extent of the cancer.

I will surrender my body to the medical personnel that attends to me. Even as I lose more and more control over my body, I will surrender it. That is, I will give it over to the One who created it in the first place. This does not mean that God will keep my body whole or reverse the decomposition. It means that by surrendering my body, I will be sharing every pain and every loss with God. I will not have to experience this ordeal alone. No question about it, cancer is a heavy burden to bear, but I will not have to bear it by myself.

I will surrender to the suffering because it is inevitable. Surely, I will opt for the treatments and medicines that may mitigate the pain, yet, I am aware that there will be some physical and mental suffering regardless of medical intervention. I have no illusions that the suffering will be easy. Courage will get me through the suffering, but it won't immunize me from it.

When I surrender control over my life, I become anxious. I am afraid, although I am not sure of what. Real or imagined control over what happens to me has provided me with a sense of security throughout my life. I have believed that lack of control leads to danger, pain, and even death. Why then would I want to give up control voluntarily? Because what I am surrendering is not control, but the illusion of control. In truth, I have no control over my life. Facing that reality can be the beginning of surrender.

When I surrender my will, which includes my preferences, my expectations, my sense of what is best for me, and my identity as a separate being; the reality of my oneness with God, and with all beings, becomes my frame of reference for living and dying.

When I surrender to the present moment I awaken to the life before me. I take back the attention I have given away to a memory or a daydream, and I attend to the reality with which I am faced.

Surrendering to now, I bring to bear my focus, my alertness, and my responsiveness to life as it unfolds moment by moment. When I surrender to now, I experience fully what is happening in real time. If I am to treat my illness and, ultimately, my death with respect and understanding; I must be wide awake and present.

In the prelude to death, I will surrender to the humiliation and indignity that accompanies terminal cancer. Loss of privacy, loss of independence, loss of control, and loss of bodily functions may all be in store for me. These losses will also necessitate loss of pride. I think I dread these losses more than I dread the physical pain. To surrender my pride will perhaps be my greatest challenge. Surrendering my pride, my self-sufficiency, and my self-image will free me to get through whatever comes my way.

In the prelude to death, I will surrender to the moment I am living. This will require that I release my hold on the way things were in the past and on the way I would prefer them to be in the future. To surrender to the present means that I am giving my full attention to what is happening now, instead of lamenting yesterday or dreading tomorrow. To surrender to the present moment empowers me because it is where I find what I need to make it through the dark night of terminal cancer.

So many people have suffered from cancer; so many are suffering now. I think of them as I await cancer's impact on me. I will think of them when I am in the worst of it. I will surrender to the suffering by being present to it, by not bracing myself against it, and by allowing it to take me deeper into communion with God.

I surrender my heart to God. Now it is the beating of God's heart that I sense within me. Now it is the love of God that I receive and pass on to the world.

I surrender my mind to God. Now I am continually God-conscious. Now it is the mind of God that prompts my thoughts. Now I remember to be mindful of the moment I am living.

I surrender my soul to God. God is the essence of my existence, the purpose of my being. I give up my life that God may live and love through me.

Dying

*The art of living well and the art of
dying well are one.*

Epicurus

Even as I took my first breath I was already
dying.

The nature of life is death and rebirth.
Without the constant death of my body at the
cellular level there could be no rebirth, no
change, no growth and development, no life. I
understand and accept that. But when it comes
to my total and complete physical death, it is a
different matter altogether.

I don't know how to die. I move toward the unknown without a clue of what will become of me. All I know is that it involves letting go, giving myself away, surrendering everything, holding nothing back.

I have never been close to my own death, but there was once when I thought I was. My young family and I were in a hotel room one morning preparing to go to Disneyland when I was suddenly struck with a severe pain that traversed my chest all the way to my back. At first I was frightened by its power to flatten me. When it persisted and worsened, the possibility that I was dying of a heart attack entered my mind.

Paramedics came rushing in to check me out; and I could see the alarm on the faces of my wife and children. What surprised me most was my response to what was happening. I was not afraid to die. I found myself praying within, not for myself, but for my family. I did not want to leave my young children fatherless and my wife a widow. Fortunately, my problem was caused by muscle spasms and not my heart. My death would wait for another day.

Years ago some friends and I experimented as a group pretending that we had one year to live. We met monthly to share our experiences. Although we came away at the end of the year with more awareness of death and appreciation of life, we were well aware that it was not the same as really living our last year. We all agreed that we benefitted individually and as a group. In retrospect, and in the light of the terminal diagnosis, I can see clearly that the main event is very different from the dress rehearsal.

It will be painful for those who love me when I die; and it will be painful for me to say goodbye to those whom I so dearly love. All the heavenly descriptions of the afterlife that I have heard pale in contrast to being with my beloved family in the here and now. Death does not terrify me; not being with my loved ones does. My greatest fear has always been that I might not be available to a loved one when he or she most needs me. To die is to be permanently unavailable. If I allow myself to dwell on that reality, my heart bleeds and I die a thousand deaths. My only recourse is to be as available as I can be while I am still alive, and to commend my loved ones to the care of one another when I am no longer here.

> *It seems that in the homestretch of our life our focal point is love; love of family and friends, love of life, and love of God. Nothing matters now except the connection of our heart. Just the thought of never again looking upon those whom we love, never again listening to their voices or embracing them, is enough to cast us into the deep abyss of sorrow and grief. And yet, this is the reality of death.* (Quezada. *Old Soul, Young Spirit: Reflections on Growing Old, 2015).*

I approach death with reverence and awe. Death is not the last period in the book of life, but merely a semicolon that portends even grander being in the heart of God. Death is not punishment; rather, it is the culmination of life as I have known it. I do not know what will happen when I die. I believe that my body, my personality, and my consciousness will cease to be; and my soul will simply be reabsorbed into the essence of God.

Death approaches, not as an enemy, but as a liberator of my soul. Death has let it be known that it is on its way. It has given me advance notice so that I may get used to the idea. It has given me the opportunity to settle my personal affairs and to help others before I go. Death is the night that calls me forth. I will not fight against it. It is as much a part of God as is the life with which I have been blessed.

My son was only seventeen years old when he was run over by a careless driver and died two days later. He was too young to die. He had his whole life ahead of him. If only we could have saved him. We were prepared to do anything to keep him alive, but that was not to be. In contrast, I am an old man now. My life is behind me. I accept the coming of death as the natural course of events. I have had my time. I have been blessed in every way.

When I taught a community college course on death and dying back in the 1980s, the curriculum included the five stages of grief that those with terminal illness experienced, according to Swiss psychiatrist Elisabeth Kubler-Ross. These stages included denial, anger, bargaining, depression, and acceptance. In those days these stages were accepted as the universal experience of those who were dying, but we have since learned that these are only some of the emotional experiences of terminally ill persons; and they don't necessarily happen in the order Kubler-Ross presented them. Because each of us is a unique individual, we each experience dying uniquely.

When my friends and family heard about my cancer diagnosis some of them told me that they had faith that I was going to be all right. I too believe that I am going to be all right – not cured of my cancer – but all right nevertheless. I don't believe that my acceptance of the pain, the suffering, and the ultimate death that come with cancer means that I don't have faith. My faith does not preclude pain and suffering, but it can help me get through the most difficult times of my life. Faith for me is not about believing in a particular outcome, but about having the wherewithal to cope with whatever comes. It is about surrendering to what is.

I must die to that which keeps me from living fully. That is, I must release that which inhibits me from embracing my humanity and being true to my basic self.

To die before I die means that I allow my false and separate self to fade into the light of my true being. The time of dying is the time to purge myself of that which keeps my spirit from soaring and my heart from loving. It is the time to dispel my illusion of self-sufficiency and to embrace my oneness with all that is. It is time to release my hold on the superficial and cling to that which is real.

To die before I die means that I give up my self-centered life so that God may live and love through me. It means to put down the extraneous load that I carry, and instead, take up matters of the soul. And finally, dying before I die is to surrender my personage and the image I have built around it, leaving only my basic self, my soul, the kernel of my essence.

Dying has more to do with life than it does with death. In fact, dying really means living my last days. Until I actually pass through the portal of death, I am still living. Essentially, I am living even as I am dying. Although I am not promised a tomorrow or even the end of today, the moment before me is filled with promise because in this moment I live and love.

As I prepare to enter fully into the experience of symptomatic cancer, I am hopeful, but my hope is not that nature will reverse its course and commute my death sentence. Rather, I am hopeful that I will be given the strength and perseverance to traverse the rough terrain that lies before me. I am hopeful that even when my heart becomes compromised by thickened blood, it will still be filled with gratitude for the life I have been granted, the human beings I have known, and the beautiful life-sustaining Earth on which I have lived. I am hopeful that those whom I leave behind will know the joy of living that I have known. May they be inspired by love and moved by compassion as they tend to one another.

Although my dying time has narrowed my scope of the world, and has me focused mostly on those within the intimate circle of my life; there is a part of me that is still conscious of the global family to which I belong. I am aware of the mass killings that are taking place daily supposedly in the name of God.

I know that millions of innocent civilians are being displaced from their homes by the ubiquitous stench of war. It is clear that our world leaders are motivated by pride, power, and property more than by the welfare of the people they lead.

I think about the children of Earth who are going without food, water, shelter, and medicine. I am grateful that there are those who try to the best of their ability to address these woeful conditions, but they are so limited in number and in power to change the status quo.

I will die without knowing why evil is so strong against the innocent creatures of God. I will never understand why we allow such disparity between those with wealth and those without. If I lived yet another lifetime I would still be lamenting the same conditions.

I know that, along with others, I have done my small part to make a better world, but sometimes it is so discouraging in the face of such powerful forces as hate, greed, and apathy.

I pass on the baton to my children and grandchildren, and to those I leave behind. May they be given the strength and courage to continue the struggle for peace and harmony within our human race. May they be armed with the weapons of love, compassion, and understanding.

Here, at the confluence of life and death, my opposites are reconciled; my shattered forces are gathered; and my oneness with God is revealed. I have been as a candle burning in the darkness that surrounds me. When my light burns out, the darkness will absorb me. I will die into the darkness; I will be the darkness.

My soul dares to live in the uncertainty of now, for that is all there is. As death approaches, my soul welcomes it. My soul is acquainted with death and does not fear it. My soul is not held to the limits of life, but moves beyond the finite to the infinite. I am so much more than my physical and mental self. My essential being transcends the boundaries of my birth and death. I am the vastness of the universe, the fathomlessness of infinity, and the perpetuity of eternity.

Journal

There is, of course, always the personal satisfaction of writing down one's own experiences so they may be saved, caught and pinned under glass, hoarded against the winter of forgetfulness. Time has been cheated a little, at least, in one's own life, and a personal, trivial immortality of an old self assured.

Anne Morrow Lindbergh

***

My hand is a little shaky as I write these words. I just got off the phone with my doctor. After evaluating my routine blood lab test he is concerned that I might have cancer of the blood and bone marrow. He wants to refer me to an oncologist.

***

There are more tests to check out, so it's not for sure. At first I was calm about it, but right now I am feeling a little shaky. I know that God is within me no matter what I have to go through in the future. I am not alone and I have the strength and courage that God has provided me. This is true regardless of my eventual diagnosis.

***

It is interesting how even vanity defers to death. I was just combing my hair and noticed that I was losing hair in the bathroom sink. At first I got worried about it, but then I had a flash of reality. Who cares about hair when they're going to die?

***

I went about my errands today. I stopped at the post office to send off some books. There was a long line of people mailing their Christmas presents. I didn't mind waiting. Suddenly I felt less of a rush in my life than I did before. As I waited, I watched all the people waiting with me. I've *always loved watching people. I thought to myself that neither they nor I have any idea how much time we have left in this physical life. One moment or one century, it is all the same. Life is life, regardless of its duration.*

***

I am aware that my wife Judy is worried about my health. She has always been so supportive of me; and she is now as well. I don't worry for myself as much as for her. She is stronger than I am in many ways, yet, I worry how it will be for her when I am gone.

***

I woke up at two o'clock this morning. I read a while and meditated. I still don't know my diagnosis so I am just coasting until I do.

***

It is interesting to me that I am not as concerned about my time running out as I am grateful that I still have some living to do. Life has been good. I have been content. My sense of it right now is that I will go through whatever is in store for me with grace and gratitude.

***

This morning I am off to my daughter Maria's classroom to talk with her fifth grade students about "kindness to strangers." It will be fun. That age group is ready to share.

***

Even if what I have is terminal, I believe that I will be okay. My difficulty will be about not being here for my loved ones, as well as for those in the community who depend on me. That will require a major letting go on my part.

***

Sunday morning I typically watch the political shows on television. It is a ritual for me. I was watching very intently this morning, but when my dog Zorro let me know that he wanted to play with me, I didn't hesitate to turn off the TV and start chasing him. He was definitely a priority.

***

I am noticing myself detaching from situations that in the past would concern me. It's not apathy that I am feeling, rather, I am just letting go of what I cannot control.

***

I received news from my doctor's office today that I need to go to a hematologist/oncologist for further evaluation and some tests. That's okay. We are moving toward a diagnosis now.

***

It is interesting to me that the things I would normally buy for myself I now consider inappropriate to buy since I probably will not be making use of them for long. When I hear people talk about future events I realize that I may or may not be here to experience them.

***

I got up at 2 a.m. – couldn't sleep. I listened to music, meditated, and then did some research on multiple myeloma. This is the cancer that my doctor suspects that I have. Okay, now I am officially scared. From what I have read, the disease sounds awful.

***

I fell asleep last night praying for the strength to face whatever the doctor's diagnosis was to be this morning. I awoke today with a heart full of gratitude. I felt grateful for so many things in my life, including the possibility that I might have cancer. I felt gratitude in general as well as for specific things. The interesting thing was that this overwhelming gratitude had overcome the fear I had been feeling yesterday. When the doctor's appointment for Friday was urgently moved up to today, I was sure something serious was going on.

***

My grateful heart carried me into the doctor's office. It was good to have Judy with me to face my new reality. She is the reason for so much of my gratitude.

***

Okay. The diagnosis came: it looks very much like multiple myeloma. I had a bone marrow biopsy to confirm the diagnosis and tomorrow I will be told how far the cancer has progressed. I had prepared myself enough so that the doctor's words would not be a shock to me.

***

The strange thing is that this incurable illness has brought about the beginning of the best chapter of my life. I know there will be pain and trouble up ahead, and then death. Yet, I am looking forward to all of it with great anticipation and gratitude. On top of it all, the oncologist that diagnosed me is one of the kindest men I have ever met. If I had to get cancer, this is the doctor that I want to help me through the coming ordeal.

***

Yesterday my oncologist called with what he considered "good news," He said that it was definitely multiple myeloma, but that its effect would be minimal at this point. He said we would just wait and watch for now.

***

Now the hard part had come. I had to begin telling my loved ones what I was facing. First, I told my grown children. Judy and I had decided it was best to call them together to tell them. We did that last night. It was very difficult at first, but their presence, their support, and their love made it all easier.

We talked, we cried, we hugged and cried some more. I told them that I felt "carried" by their presence and support. It was as if they were sharing this burden with me. Perhaps they were carrying the heavier part.

Today I begin to tell others: my brother and sisters, and my friends.

***

I went to call my best friend Roy today to let him know what is happening in my life. He and I have been friends since the fifth grade, and we have always had each other's back. He was with me as my best man when I was married, and he was with me at the funeral of my son. Before I even took a step toward the phone, reality hit me square in the face – Roy died two months ago. The memory of his friendship sustains me, but just now I would really like to talk with him.

***

When I experienced my family's response to my diagnosis, I realized that my death will affect their lives dramatically and will bring much pain and disruption, grief and sorrow. Their anticipatory bereavement prompted mine as well. I began to grieve all that would be lost to me by dying.

***

As I anticipate the progression of my cancer, I am aware of the losses that are coming. This illness will be teaching me a level of humility that I would prefer not to learn. I know that the privacy I demand now, the dignity to which I cling, and the self-sufficiency with which I pride myself, will probably go by the wayside. But I'm sure I will have bigger problems than those with which to be concerned.

***

I feel as though I am beginning a new life, at least a new chapter of my life – the most important one.

***

I have to admit that I am dreading the physical pain ahead, but I try not to spend too much mental time on that. It will be my focus soon enough and it doesn't have to be now.

***

At the core of my being I want to befriend my cancer; I want to welcome this dying time. I don't want to approach this challenge as a war against the illness or death. They are not the enemy as far as I'm concerned. They are part of the natural process of life. We don't fight against our birth, why should we do battle with our death? I want to live the rest of my life wholeheartedly and I want to do my dying wholeheartedly.

***

Yesterday was a day of love. I began telling my friends and extended family the news. There was an outpouring of genuine love from so many. I was overwhelmed and exhausted by the end of the day. Some people wanted me to get a second opinion; some wanted me to fight the diagnosis; some understood my response to cancer. Some gave me recommendations for doctors they knew about; others wanted me to "go organic." All I wanted was for them to hear it from me rather than second hand. I know they all meant well.

***

When I am not praying, that is, experiencing the God of my soul, I feel as though I am sinking into the water. When I pray, I am lifted up, I am encouraged, and I am all right. As I began to pray this morning, I heard these words deep within me: "Let go."

***

Yesterday afternoon I went to see my friend Lavern. I told her about my cancer and she turned white. She told me that she had dreamt a month ago that I had cancer. Her late husband Joe was in the dream. Lavern said that Joe said to me in the dream, "...well at least you didn't die."

***

Judy and I continue to talk about living with terminal illness and living with dying. Our communication is good. We are becoming even closer than we already were. Calls from my family members continue to come.

***

The thickening of my blood caused by the cancer may be slowing down my heart, but it has not stopped my heart from pumping out the courage that I need to stay afloat.

***

I have not written in this journal for a while, yet, so much has happened. The reality of this cancer seems so far off that it has allowed me to detach from it. I know that it is real and that it is going to make me very sick and eventually kill me. But my overriding reality today is that I am healthy and I am happy, contented, and at peace with myself and with the world. I am not alone as I go forward, but I am heart-broken for those who must suffer alone. May they come to know the solace that comes from those who care.

***

I awoke at two this morning. I was dreaming of my sister Mary Helen again. I am not sure what she signifies for me. I know she was kind, innocent, helpful, and simple. I know she died of cancer. Maybe it will be her spirit that will somehow accompany me through the darkness and into the light. It is comforting to imagine it.

***

Today I am thinking about the dreams for the future that I have had. They will have to be set aside now in light of the diagnosis. I used to dream about someday owning land and spending my last days there. I used to dream about travelling to places like Italy. Those dreams no longer fit into my life. Pretty much what I have is all I get; and that's all right with me. I have a lot and it will serve me well from here to the end of my life.

***

I had lunch with my friend John yesterday. We always have a good time visiting. We eat delicious salmon at Rincon Market and talk about politics, religion, and life. Then I went to visit my friend Fr. Bob Fuller. He is doing well right now, but we don't know from day-to-day if that will last. I suppose that is true for all of us. I was so humbled when Fr. Bob asked me the other day if I would give a eulogy at his funeral. Of course I said yes, but later we laughed together as we wondered who was going to outlive whom.

***

My oncologist just informed me that my diagnosis has changed from multiple myeloma to Waldenstrom macroglobulinemia. Instead of the bones and bone marrow being affected, it is the blood and bone marrow.

***

I am determined not to be treated for my cancer. I am willing to do what it takes to manage the illness, but nothing that will kill my immune system. The oncologist will tell me in a few days how the thickness of my blood is. I won't see him again for months. I feel fatigue sometimes. I don't know what symptoms to attribute to my cancer and which ones to attribute to old age.

***

Today my oncologist called to tell me that my protein, which causes thickening of my blood is higher than it was two weeks ago. That is not good news. I was told only days ago that I would not have to worry about symptoms for a long time, but I guess that's not really true. Doctors just guess about those things like the rest of us.

***

I am getting ready to go to bed. I hear an owl hooting nearby. Her haunting call in the night seems appropriate somehow.

***

This morning I find myself thinking about priorities. In my counseling practice I would sometimes have clients set their priorities by a process of elimination. I would ask them to list the five most important things to them (health, work, family, etc.). Then I would ask them to consider the list and then eliminate one of the five from their life. Then I would ask them to give up another and another until they were left with one.

That one would be their number one priority, the one they dropped before that would be number two, and so on. Next, I would ask the clients to list their priorities again according to their priority number, then to consider how much of their time and energy they spent in any given day with each priority. The results were sometimes quite revealing, especially when their top priority received little to none of their time and energy. The idea was to become conscious of spending the appropriate time and energy on those things they valued most. I encouraged them to be congruent between what they valued most and the way they lived their life.

As I do this exercise today, in the light of the terminal diagnosis, my priorities in order of importance to me are: <u>God</u> – staying conscious of the essence of God, praying and meditating, and spending time in solitude; <u>family</u> – spending time with family, being for them, loving and being loved; <u>physical health</u> – staying in shape, exercising, eating right, resting, adequate sleep; <u>work</u> – writing, counseling others, household *responsibilities; and <u>friends</u> – visiting with friends, corresponding with them.*

***

Today I went on a long walk with my son Miguel. We do that often. Our walks give us a chance to catch up on things. Today we walked into a wooded area that I like to frequent. Deep in the thatch of mesquite trees there is a special place where I want my ashes scattered when the time comes. I took advantage of this opportunity to show Miguel that place. He took note. Although difficult, those things need to be talked about.

***

There are ordinary events that take on extraordinary qualities when experienced in the light of a terminal diagnosis. Today was such an event. It is Easter Sunday at our house and my children and their families were here to celebrate life together. There was a lot of good food shared, stories told, laughter heard, and even a full-fledged Easter egg hunt that even the young adult grandchildren insisted on having. What was the most special for me was that my grandchildren spontaneously gathered at my table. We got to talking about politics, the news media, and even about dating. It was such a joy conversing with them, and even more of a joy just being with them. There seems to be an unspoken realization among us that these gatherings may be numbered.

***

As I observe people walking down the street or working out at the gym, I realize that just as they don't know that I have cancer, I also don't know what, if anything, ails them. I don't know what others are walking with as they make the best of their lives in spite of their circumstances.

***

God is in my healthy cells; God is in my unhealthy cells; God is in what gives me life; God is in what kills me.

***

There is a big difference between fear of suffering during the dying time and fear of death itself.

***

I won't run away from death, but I won't run toward it either. Dying from a terminal illness is a slow walk toward the inevitable with time enough to pray.

***

How can I find beauty in dying when dying is marked by the ugliness of disintegration? If I can love dying as much as I love living, then dying will take on the beauty of love.

***

God fills me with love and life right when I need it most. It occurs to me this morning that I may be losing everything I cherish; yet, even death does not; cannot; will not; deprive me of being with God.

***

I do not believe in afterlife retribution for sins committed or in reward for a good life lived. I do not believe in the continuation of my physical or psychological self after death. My soul, that is, my essential being, will simply return to the Essence of God from whence it came.

***

It dawned on me today that I still have time to offer my services to others. There is a program that I put together some time ago that I could make available to persons like myself who find themselves facing the issues of old age, illness, and imminent death. This is something I don't need to do, but it is in my nature to want to do it.

***

Sometimes I feel guilty because there are so many people actually suffering from cancer in the world today. Some are terminal, some are not; but, in any case, they are hurting badly. And here I am, writing about a terminal cancer diagnosis and its effects on my life even before the first serious symptom makes an appearance. It doesn't seem fair that I have been granted this grace period and they have not.

***

In the prelude to my death I will seek reconciliation where there has been rift. I will ask forgiveness and offer it too. I will accept what is inevitable. I will know life as I have never known it. I will die before I die. I will commune with the earth and all creation. I will offer my love, service, and compassion. I will honor endings, and celebrate the passing of the torch.

***

Martin Luther said that if he knew that today was to be the last day of his life, he would still plant a tree. I too must plant a tree before I die - however close or far away that day may be. Imminent death is not a reason for me to stop living or creating or contributing to the world. On the contrary, it is the impetus for investing all that I can for the good of others. To plant a tree is to live life to the fullest within my limitations. To plant a tree is to give form to whatever is in my heart. It is to promote the welfare of others, whoever they may be. I will continue to invest in my life and in the lives of others, even if I will not be a part of their future. I will invest in life until my last breath.

***

I think of the gorgeous desert sunset that blazes its hues of red, blue, green, and yellow into the dying of the light; one last manifestation of beauty before it disappears into the night.

Before the Night Comes

Before the night comes may I embrace the reality of my poverty. May I realize that all my possessions are nothing in the light of impermanence. May I release my hold on power, comfort, and security, for these are but illusions in the realm of the soul. May I accept my indigence as the human condition that allows me to receive the gifts of life and death.

Before the night comes may I grieve with all my heart for that which I am losing. May I be given the strength to let go of whom and what I have known and cherished. May I relinquish my false self so that my essential self may flourish. And may I leave the legacy of love in the wake of my existence.

Before the night comes may I see myself through the eyes of God. May I accept myself for who I am; no more, no less. May I be grounded in the ordinary and espouse the commonplace. May I take my place among the least of us and the most despised. And may I accept humiliation as a privilege and suffering as a sacrifice.

Before the night comes may I be emptied of that which kills my spirit, and filled with that which sustains my soul. May I yearn for God alone as my source and destiny. May all my intentions fall away save these: to love the world with all my heart; to seek and do the universal good; to pray for those I leave behind; and to commend my soul to the ultimate union of all that is.

Before the night comes may I repent of my iniquities and be willing to be forgiven. May I free my debtors from the chains of my resentments, and release the rancor from my heart. May what I think and what I do be grounded in the soil of mercy for myself and for those whose lives I touch.

Before the night comes may my heart be cleansed and purified by the grace I don't deserve. May my heart be open to holy love, and my eyes behold the face of God in everyone I meet. May my soul abide in the heart of God now and evermore; and may my glimpse of God inspire me to be a servant to the world.

Before the night comes may I have the courage to live fully and authentically, regardless of the consequences. May I speak the words that must be spoken and do the things that must be done, even in the face of opposition or the certainty of contempt. May my heart be brave and my mind be resolute in living out my truth.

Before the night comes may I be grateful for all that life has given me. May I appreciate the good and the bad, the mountains and the valleys, the days of light and the days of darkness. May I be thankful to all who journeyed with me; and may the joy of having lived and loved be ever in my soul. (Quezada. *Of Mind and Spirit, 2014).*

Appendix A

Waldenstrom macroglobulinemia (WM) is a rare, incurable lymphoma, a cancer of the blood and bone marrow. Between 1,000 and 1,500 cases of WM are diagnosed each year in the United States. WM usually affects male patients in their seventh decade of life, although it can also affect younger men and women, but that is unusual. No definitive cause has been identified for WM.

The over production of protein in the blood causes the blood to thicken and consequently causes the heart to work harder to pump the blood. Because the heart works harder and the blood flows slower, heart failure may result, as well as damage to the kidneys, and other organs. Other symptoms of WM include: oozing of the blood from the nose and gums, blurred vision, headaches, vertigo, retinal vein engorgement, stupor, recurrent infections, weakness, fatigue, anemia, weight loss, severe neuropathy, fever, night sweats, gastrointestinal tract problems, and enlarged lymph nodes and spleen and/or liver. WM may also cause new cancers, including multiple myeloma.

Because WM has a slow progression, no treatment is recommended until symptoms begin to appear. When treatment does become necessary, its purpose is strictly for symptom control and to prevent organ damage.

Median survival rate for WM patients is from five to eight years from diagnosis. It may be less than five years or more than eight, depending on the progression of the disease.

Author

Adolfo Quezada, a retired counselor and psychotherapist, has written eighteen books on psycho-spiritual issues. He holds master's degrees in counseling and in journalism from the University of Arizona. Quezada is married and has four children and five grandchildren. He lives in Tucson, Arizona.

Made in the USA
San Bernardino, CA
17 July 2016